# Biography
# of an Octopus

## by Alice L. Hopf

## illustrated by Mamoru Funai

## G. P. Putnam's Sons    New York

*For*
*Theo and Marie*

Text copyright © 1971 by Alice L. Hopf
Illustrations copyright © 1971 by Mamoru Funai
All rights reserved. Published simultaneously in
Canada by Longmans Canada Limited, Toronto.
*Library of Congress Catalog Card Number: 72-147283*
PRINTED IN THE UNITED STATES OF AMERICA

In a narrow crevice behind some rocks a mother octopus had made her nest. The rocks were in shallow water near the shore. But they were deep enough so that they would not be exposed at low tide.

The mother octopus had found the smallest opening among the rocks. Inside was a little cave. She had cleaned out the cave and brought more stones to pile up around the hole. Now she had a nice, safe place to lay her eggs.

The eggs were very small. They were each about the size and shape of a grain of rice. The mother octopus glued them together in long clusters, which she stuck to the sides of the cave. There were almost a thousand eggs in each cluster and the mother octopus laid more than twenty clusters. It took her two weeks to build her nest and lay her eggs, and then she settled down to brood them.

An octopus is a devoted mother. It took almost seven weeks for the eggs to hatch. All that time, the mother octopus stood guard in her hole. She tended her eggs carefully. Sometimes she cradled them in her arms. She caressed them with her tentacles so that no dirt or fungus could get onto them. She squirted them with water from her siphon so that they would stay fresh and clean.

Every octopus has a siphon, a tube that sticks out through a slit in its skin. From the siphon it can squirt out water or ink. The octopus head is attached to its baglike body with hardly any neck between. In the center of its head the octopus has a hard, beaklike mouth, something like a parrot's beak. The eyes are raised on knobs so that it can see all around.

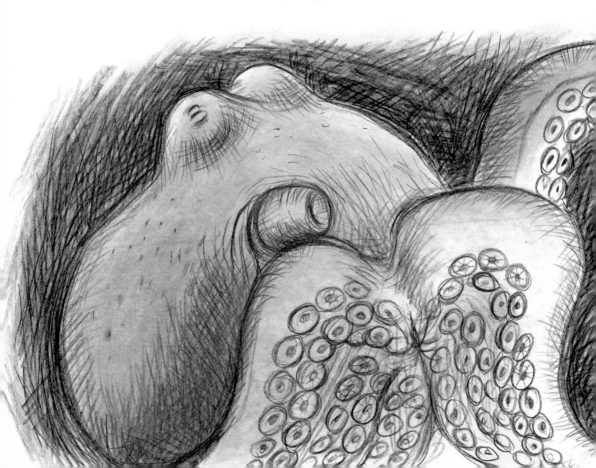

When the mother octopus peered out of the narrow mouth of her cave, it was not to catch a passing fish. She was watching for the approach of an enemy. She was on guard to be sure no sea animal would eat or hurt her eggs. If a fish or a crab or even another octopus came near, she waved her tentacles threateningly. If it did not go away, she rushed out to the attack.

The eggs were transparent. Inside, the baby octopuses could be seen moving about. Sometimes they changed color. Little spots of orange-brown appeared and disappeared on the tiny bodies inside the eggs.

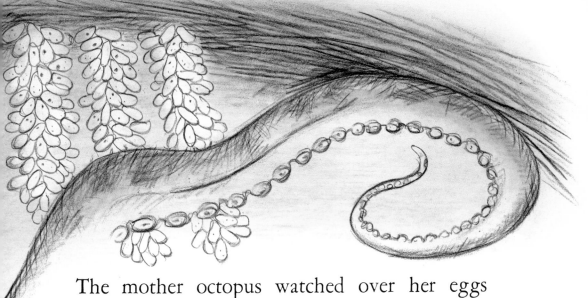

The mother octopus watched over her eggs for almost 50 days. By that time she was much thinner, for she had hardly eaten anything at all. Only a few times did she leave her nest at night to find food. At last the little eggs began to hatch. One after another the babies broke the skin of the eggs. They were almost tiny copies of their mother and could swim and squirt ink just as she could.

Each little octopus had a round head from which eight tiny arms extended. The arms were so little that they seemed more like a circlet of hairs around the head.

The baby octopuses floated toward the surface of the water. One of the last of the babies to leave the cave was a strong little male. We shall call him Ollie. (His scientific name is *Octopus vulgaris*.) He squeezed out of his egg skin to the top of the cave and out through a chink in the stones.

Little Ollie floated into the upper layer of ocean water. The sun warmed the water and gave him life and energy. He floated in what is called the plankton layer. It is made of thousands of tiny sea creatures. The ocean currents scattered the baby octopuses far and wide. Only a few would live to grow up. Most would be eaten by other sea animals.

Ollie was a strong, alert octopus baby. He was able to catch the smallest plankton creatures when he was hungry. But he was able to escape the bigger ones that wanted to eat *him*. He grew bigger and stronger every day. His short little arms grew longer. He could reach farther. He could catch bigger creatures to eat.

At last he grew big enough to move down through the water and begin living on the bottom of the ocean. When he saw a sandy spot among some rocks, he squirted water from his little siphon. This made him shoot backward through the water. He darted down to the opening among the rocks. He reached out with two of his arms and his suckers took hold of the stones. Two more of his arms went down to feel the sand. Soon he was walking along the sea bottom, using his arms like legs.

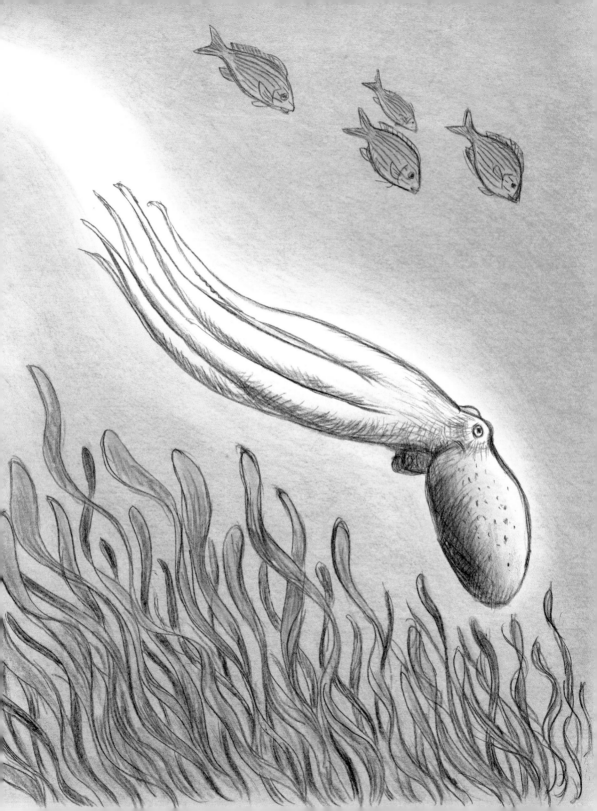

Ollie explored this new place he had found. It was a good place for an octopus to live. Ollie found a little hole under a rock. He hid in the hole and peered out at the other creatures in the sea. When a tiny crab went by, Ollie reached out with an arm and grabbed it. The suckers on his arm clamped tightly to the crab. It could not get away. Ollie pulled it into his den and ate it.

He was also fond of crayfish and mussels. Sometimes he collected several mussels before he had a meal. He fastened the suckers of his arms onto the two shells of the mussel. Then he pulled them apart and ate the animal inside. When he was done, he left a pile of little shells outside his hole.

Ollie soon learned how to catch all the food he needed. Sometimes he sneaked up on a crab quietly. He used his eight arms like feet to pull him along the ocean bottom. As he reached out with an arm for a rock and clamped his suckers onto it, he released the suckers on his arms that were holding him to the rock behind. Ollie moved sideways when he walked this way.

Sometimes he shot toward the surface by squirting water downward from his siphon. From above he watched the rocks and the sand below. When he saw a crayfish, he spread out his arms till the web of skin connecting them looked like an umbrella. With this parachute, he floated quietly down upon his prey. The crayfish could not escape from underneath.

Sometimes he floated just above the bottom and walked on tiptoe, with his tentacles hardly touching the sand. When he saw something good to eat, he reached out a long arm and clamped his suckers on it.

Ollie found plenty of food among the rocks and pools near his home. But there were also bigger creatures that would like to eat him. His worst enemy was the moray eel. Ollie knew by instinct just what to do when one was near. Sometimes he crouched on a rock where he could see all around him. His color became just like the rock. His skin poked up in little warts like the barnacles on the rocks behind him. He was almost invisible.

But moray eels have good eyes. They are used to looking for octopuses. When an eel came very close to Ollie, he left his rock. He shot away fast with his jet propulsion. At the same time, he changed color. He was no longer brown like the rock. He was a white ghost octopus, almost the color of the water he swam in.

Ollie had still another defense. He shot ink out of his siphon tube. A cloud of black octopus ink came out in front of the eel's hungry snout. It was almost the same size and shape as Ollie. The eel snapped at this black cloud that looked like an octopus. He didn't know where the real octopus had gone. But the white, ghostlike Ollie was far away, hiding in a crack in the rocks.

Ollie could change to any color that he wanted. When he was angry, he turned red. When he was frightened, he became white. When he wanted to look like a rock or the sandy sea bottom, he changed color to match. Sometimes he even had stripes or spots. Ollie showed how he was feeling by the color of his skin. When disturbed, he could change color quickly and waves of blue, gray, red, white, or orange would wash across his body.

One day Ollie found an old bottle half buried in the sand. He just managed to squeeze inside. Nothing big could get in to hurt him. It was like a new home.

And then a strange thing happened. The bottle began to rise off the ocean floor. Ollie looked out through the glass and saw a huge, strange creature. It had big eyes and long legs. It was a skin diver. It was Ollie's first meeting with a man.

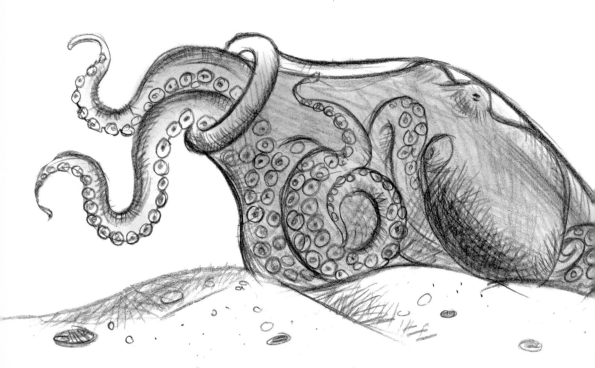

Ollie changed colors fast. He shot up to the top of the bottle and out the narrow neck. When the skin diver made a grab for him, he let out a cloud of ink. He shot away from that place as fast as he could go.

Ollie was frightened. He thought only of getting away from that terrible creature. And since octopuses must travel backward, he did not look where he was going. Ollie shot right past a hungry moray eel! By the time Ollie saw him, it was too late to do anything but dodge. He had used up most of his ink on the skin diver.

The eel struck with his mouth wide and his sharp teeth ready to bite. Ollie dodged aside, but the eel grabbed hold of one of his arms. Ollie tugged. The eel tugged. Ollie's other arms seized hold of a rock. The suckers held. Ollie turned red with anger. He gave a strong, hard pull.

Suddenly he was free. His arm had broken off, leaving the hungry eel with only a part of an octopus arm to eat. Ollie hurriedly hid himself under the rocks and sand.

When the eel had gone away, Ollie went back to his little cave. He stayed there for a long time. He pulled rocks and shells around the opening so that the eel could not get in. He waited quietly for crabs or shrimp to go past his door. In six weeks, he had grown a new part for his broken arm. It was as strong and supple as the old one and had the same number of suckers. His arm was like new.

Ollie stayed near home for a long time after that. Little by little he forgot his narrow escape. And as he grew larger he could catch bigger prey.

He discovered a new animal that tasted good. Quietly he floated in the water, watching the rocks for lobsters. Quickly he parachuted down upon them. He learned to keep away from their big claws that could pinch his arms. Ollie had a special method for subduing lobsters or crabs. He ejected a poison from his mouth that paralyzed the creature. When it could no longer pinch him with its claws, he wrapped his tentacles around it. He fastened his suckers to the legs and the shells and pulled them apart. He had a tasty meal.

One day Ollie found a strange thing lying on the sand in the sea. It was round and had an opening like a cave. Inside he found four big lobsters.

Ollie had never seen so many lobsters in one place. It was a feast indeed! He prepared to stay for several days. First he ejected his poison and paralyzed all the lobsters. Then one by one he pulled them apart. He ate all the good meat. In between lobsters he rested. Then he ate some more.

Ollie was eating the last lobster when the thing began to rise up out of the water. This time he did not shoot out of the hole and get away. He was too full of lobster. Also he did not want to give up the last of this good food.

Ollie was caught in a lobster pot! It was jerked quickly out of the water and into a fisherman's boat. All the water drained out of it. For the first time Ollie was in open air instead of in the sea. He wrapped his arms around the inside of the trap. He held fast with his suckers, glaring up at the fisherman who looked into the pot.

"Well now," cried the fisherman. "What have we here? A thief in the pot — and he's eaten all the lobsters! One . . . two . . . three . . . there must have been four lobsters I caught, and he's eaten them all! He'll have to pay for them, that's what! Nobody gets away with stealing Old Ben's lobsters. If I can't sell the lobsters, I'll have to sell the octopus."

The fisherman rummaged around in his boat till he found a piece of canvas. He tied the canvas around the trap so that Ollie could not get out. An octopus can live for a while out of water. But the fisherman thought it might be better to keep his captive wet. He put the canvas package in his live bait box at the back of the boat. There it could lie in the water, but the octopus could not get out.

Ollie had never been out of the water before. Even as the trap was put into the bait box, he knew something dreadful had happened. He was shut up and he was very frightened. But after a while he began to try to get out. An octopus can get out of almost anything. It can squeeze through a hole that is half its size. Ollie crawled out of the pot. Then he squeezed around underneath the canvas cover. He pushed and pulled until he found his way among the folds and out into the water in the bait box. There were fish and shrimp in the box. But Ollie wasn't hungry now. And he did not like being in the dark bait box. He crawled up to the top and out through the crack under the lid. He sat on the top of the bait box and looked around.

The boat chugged into the harbor. When the
fisherman tied up at the wharf and turned to
get his catch out of the bait box, there was Ollie
staring at him from the top of the box. The
fisherman blinked.

"By Jimminy! You're a magician for sure!" he said. "And a fine specimen now that I get a good look at you. I know who'll give me enough money for you to make up for all the lobsters you ate!"

The fisherman got a glass jar with a tight lid. He filled it with water and put Ollie in it. Ollie wanted to shoot away as he did in the sea. But he found that he could not move very fast in this strange place. The man grabbed him up and, although Ollie wrapped his arms around the hand and tried to bite, the man shoved him into the jar and screwed on the lid. Ollie glared at him through the glass. He was so mad that he changed color a dozen times. But there was nothing he could do.

The fisherman took Ollie to a scientist who worked in a marine laboratory. The scientist was studying all the animals that live in the sea. He was very glad to get Ollie and he paid the fisherman well.

The scientist put Ollie in a tank with sea water and rocks and seaweed. He tried to make it a place where an octopus would be happy. He put a fine netting over the top. He fastened it tightly. He knew how an octopus can get out of almost anything.

At first Ollie hid under a rock. He wouldn't
come out to be looked at. At night he came out
and tried to find a way to escape. He crawled
all around the tank. He crawled all across the
netting. He could not find a place big enough
to squeeze through.

After a while, Ollie got used to living in the tank. He saw that the man with the white coat did not hurt him when he looked into the tank. In fact, the man brought him good things to eat. Ollie began to come out of his hole when he saw the white coat. Then a nice shrimp or crab would be dropped into the water for him.

One day the scientist was very busy. He did not feed Ollie when he first came in. He walked back and forth at his work. Ollie was hungry. No crabs had been dropped into his tank. He crawled up onto the highest rock and watched the man. At last he could wait no longer. When the scientist walked past his tank, Ollie shot a stream of water out of his siphon. It hit the white coat right in the middle. The scientist was soaked. He was also surprised.

"Well, well! So you want some attention!" he said. "I guess I forgot your breakfast this morning."

And the man brought a handful of shrimp and dropped them into the tank.

After that, if Ollie did not get fed soon enough, he never failed to shoot water at the white coat. And the man didn't mind when he got wet.

"That's a smart little octopus I've got there," he would tell his friends. "Got a good aim, too. Never misses."

After he had said this to several people, the scientist had an idea.

"You're such a smart octopus," he told Ollie, "I'm going to give you an intelligence test. I wonder just where you will rank on the scale."

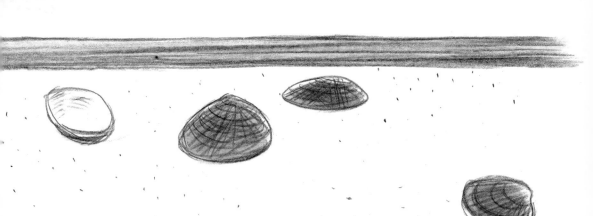

So the scientist made his preparations. He put
a little white plate into Ollie's tank. It had a
wire fastened to it and the wire conducted elec-
tricity. The plate could give a little electric
shock. Ollie would feel the shock but it would
not harm him. Then a fine, tasty crab was put
down onto the white plate.

Ollie saw the white plate. He saw the tasty crab. He was hungry. He rushed out of his den in the rocks and grabbed the crab. At once he felt the electric shock. He dropped the crab. He turned white and red with fear and anger. He fled back to his den. Ollie did not like the electric shock at all. He refused to come out for the rest of the day.

But the next morning he was hungrier. There was a crab waiting for him to eat. Ollie crawled out and got it. Nothing happened. He took it into his den and ate it. Then he looked out for another.

There was another crab out there. But there was also the white plate beside it. Ollie crawled out cautiously. He reached out with a long arm. He took hold of the crab. He got a shock.

Ollie dropped the crab and rushed back into his den. All day he sat there, white and shaken. He would not come out as long as the white plate was near. He forgot about eating. He only remembered the pain of the shock.

The next day he still remembered. He would not eat if the white plate was around. The scientist wrote it all down in his notebook. For several days the white plate was taken away and Ollie came out to eat the crabs. Then the plate was put back. If Ollie remembered, he stayed in his den. If he forgot, he came out and got a shock. He was able to remember for a longer and longer time. Soon he could remember for a whole week.

The scientist made notes and wrote a paper.

"You have a high IQ for an octopus," he said to Ollie. "Ollie, you have shown that you have a brain. I will write about you for a scientific journal. Other biologists will be interested in my experiment!"

But it's not easy to keep an octopus alive in captivity.

"I wouldn't like anything to happen to you," the scientist said one day. "Since you've been helpful to me, I believe you deserve to go back home."

Late that afternoon the scientist went for a ride in his boat. He took Ollie with him in a glass jar. When he thought he was about where the fisherman had caught the octopus, he stopped the boat. He opened the jar and let Ollie slide out into the sea.

Ollie floated for just a moment on the top of the water. Then he gathered his arms together and shot water out of his siphon. He darted away into the ocean depths. The scientist waved his hand and started the boat's motor.

Ollie went down deep into the sea. Once again he could swim as far as he wanted in any direction. There was no glass tank to keep him in one place. Soon he found a hole among the rocks. He hid himself inside.

Each day he brought more stones to protect the entrance. Each day he ate shell fish and left their shells outside. He would grow and become stronger and catch even bigger prey. He might even win a fight with an eel. But even a very smart octopus could make the mistake of crawling into a lobster trap again.

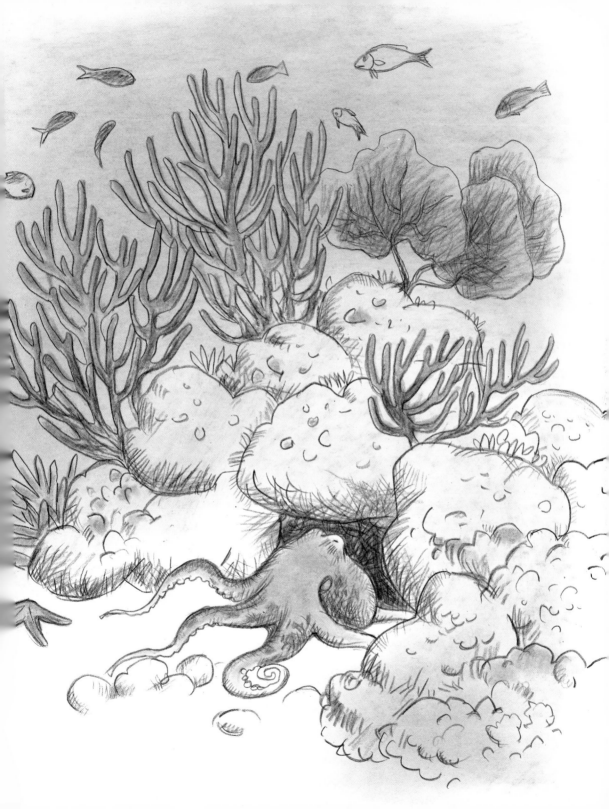

## About the Author

Alice L. Hopf is equally at home writing science fiction (under her maiden name, A. M. Lightner) and writing about nature. She is a member of the Lepidopterists Society, the New York Entomological Society, and the Audubon Society. For Putnam's she has written two other science books for young readers: *Butterfly and Moth* and *Carab the Trap-Door Spider*. Mrs. Hopf lives with her husband in New York City.

## About the Artist

Mamoru Funai was born in Hawaii and, after showing an early interest in art, attended the Honolulu Academy of Arts, the Art Institute of Pittsburgh, and the Cleveland Institute of Art. He now lives in New Jersey with his wife and their two young sons. Mr. Funai is a well-known illustrator of children's books, and has previously illustrated *Little Sponge Fisherman* and *Living in Navajoland* for Putnam's.